Neuro-Linguistic Programming

in a week

MO SHAPIRO

Hodder Arnold

A MEMBER OF THE HODDER HEADLINE GROUP

The publisher has used its best endeavours to ensure that the URLs for external websites referred to in this book are correct and active at the time of going to press. However, the publisher and the author have no responsibility for the websites and can make no guarantee that a site will remain live or that the content will remain relevant, decent or appropriate.

Order queries: please contact Bookpoint Ltd, 130 Milton Park, Abingdon, Oxon OX14 4SB. Telephone: (44) 01235 827720. Fax: (44) 01235 400454. Lines are open from 9.00–17.00, Monday to Saturday, with a 24 hour message answering service. You can also order through our website www.hoddereducation.com

British Library Cataloguing in Publication Data
A catalogue record for this title is available from the British Library

ISBN-10: 0 340 85029 9
ISBN-13: 9780340850299

First published 1998
Impression number   10   9   8   7   6
Year   2007 2006

Typeset by SX Composing DTP, Rayleigh, Essex.
Printed in Great Britain for Hodder Education, a division of Hodder Headline, 338 Euston Road, London NW1 3BH
by Cox & Wyman Ltd., Reading.

Hodder Headline's policy is to use papers that are natural, renewable and recyclable products and made from wood grown in sustainable forests. The logging and manufacturing processes are expected to conform to the environmental regulations of the country of origin.

■■■■■C O N T E N T S■■■■■

Welcome to the world of Neuro-Linguistic Programming (NLP). This book will introduce you to the main themes and ideas that constitute NLP. It will give you an outline knowledge and understanding of the key concepts accompanied by practical and thought-provoking exercises. NLP has its own language and organising systems which are fully explained, with examples which relate to work and personal issues. The theories and practice of NLP will help you discover what makes some people excel in all aspects of their lives, and will enable you to do the same.

The first time I heard about NLP, I was inclined to dismiss it as just another quick-fix system. Then one day I was travelling to meet my sister at the local station in a town 50 miles away. I had looked at the map and could see roughly the location. Confidently, I set off. As I approached the town, I began to feel uneasy. I did not know the scale of the map and was becoming unsure of my bearings. In desperation, I found someone to ask the way. She started to tell me the route and when she saw the puzzled look on my face, she decided to draw the instructions. When she had finished, I had a very detailed map, verbal descriptions of every landmark and a clear sense of where I was going. She had helped me by recognising my confusion and calming me down. This enabled me to understand and digest the information I needed. I drove to the station wondering whether she realised she was using NLP techniques.

As you go through this book, you will be able to recognise that the helper in the above passage established rapport, used sensory-based language, paced my mood and led me to a more resourceful state of mind. This is the attraction of NLP. It stems from what people do naturally, identifies what they're doing and how they are doing it so that they have increased choices in all aspects of their lives. Once you recognise the patterns and habits in your behaviour you can decide which help or hinder your life. NLP is intended to be flexible.

This book will provide explanations and a synopsis of the key concepts on Sunday. Each day of the week then represents a part of the whole NLP message and practical ideas for application. You decide in which order you want to organise your week. Take time to assimilate the concepts on each day before starting a different one. By the end of the week you will be able to use NLP at work and in your personal life in a way that will sharpen your skills and boost your achievements.

Sunday	What is Neuro-Linguistic Programming?
Monday	Personal and working beliefs
Tuesday	Knowing yourself and others
Wednesday	What exactly do you mean?
Thursday	Filter systems
Friday	Levels of change and reframing
Saturday	Increase your options

What is Neuro-Linguistic Programming?

NLP has been growing in popularity since the mid-1970s. It has many applications in the fields of communication, commerce, personal development and psychotherapy.

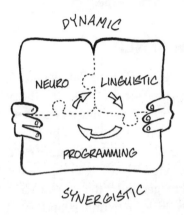

Neuro-Linguistic Programming provides a model that enhances understanding of:

Neuro — your thinking processes, the way you use your senses of sight, hearing, feeling, taste and smell to understand what is happening around you

Linguistic — your words, the way you use language and how it influences you and those around you

Programming — your behaviour and the way you organise your ideas and actions, which produces expected and unexpected results.

The way you think affects the internal and external language you use and the concepts you hold. This in turn affects the way you behave. It is a dynamic and synergistic process: the whole is greater than the sum of the parts. Any internal or external change to any of the components will have an impact on the whole.

An overview of NLP

NLP was developed by Richard Bandler and John Grinder in the early 1970s as they set out to identify the patterns used by outstanding therapists who achieved excellent results with clients. They discovered a number of processes which they fitted into an accessible model to enhance effective communication, personal change and personal development. They attempted to 'get under the skin' of Virginia Satir, Fritz Perls and Milton Erickson to understand both how they reached their levels of excellence and how to reproduce their skills. Bandler and Grinder wanted to be able to communicate and work with people as effectively as possible. They used their path to discovery as a way of showing others how to achieve success too. They began to develop NLP by doing it.

Basic principles

One of the key drivers at the core of Bandler and Grinder's work was to discover how people excel, and most particularly when managing change. With this information, they devised processes to teach those methods to others. Their studies indicated that certain basic principles needed to be in place to create the 'difference that makes the difference'. At first these may seem untenable, even awkward.

Take a few moments to imagine how you might approach situations if you accepted and worked within the principles below. What would it be like if you presupposed these principles to be true? Be curious, and rather than dismissing ideas that don't fit with yours, notice how these principles could strengthen your communications.

> ### Basic principles of excellence
>
> - We have all the resources we need
> - The meaning of any communication is the effect it has
> - There is no failure, only feedback
> - The map is not the territory: every person's map is unique

We have all the resources we need

At various points in our life, we have achieved success. The findings of NLP suggest that if we recall the ways we did so, then we can transfer these to any present-day challenges. Imagine reaching that longed-for senior position in your place of work. After the initial euphoria, you may wonder what you have let yourself in for. By remembering *how* you successfully managed changes in the past and reinserting those resources as you reach this elevated position, you can continue with confidence and anticipate fulfilment. Whether you need confidence, energy, strength or any other personal resource, be assured that you have used it somewhere in your past and can access it again.

The meaning of any communication is the effect it has

What happens when you talk or write to someone and the reply you receive is completely unexpected in content? Sometimes, you will assume that they are being awkward or ignorant in not responding the way you want. As long as you put the onus on them to somehow achieve your interpretation of what is 'right', you cannot change things. However, once you understand your own part in the equation, you can consider doing something different to put across your intended message.

> Colleagues were discussing a fractious decision-making meeting that had just ended. The final decision was made by voting after lengthy discussions to help four 'undecideds' cast their vote and press the 'yes' or 'no' button. 'How did you eventually decide?' Terry asked Sarah. 'I listened to all the arguments and then imagined how they would work in my department.' 'No. *How* did you *decide*?' A confused Sarah answered, speaking slowly: 'I listened to all the arguments and then imagined how they would work in my department.' As Terry was about to ask his question a third time, Ashra translated: 'Which way did you cast your vote?'

There is no failure, only feedback
How do you react when, in your opinion, things go wrong? Are you a tryer who persists in doing the same thing over and over until, if ever, you get it right? Or do you think it over, and decide what you can do differently for a better result next time? Think about a time in the past when you know you made a mistake. Imagine calling yourself a failure. What does that look or sound like? How do you feel? Now imagine the same situation and ask yourself 'What could I have done differently to achieve what I wanted?' What does that look or sound like? How do you feel? The notion of learning from

feedback means that you are more likely to be flexible rather than rigid in your dealings with yourself and others.

Remember: if what you're doing isn't working, do something else.

Thomas Edison, when called a failure for taking so long to invent the light bulb, responded: 'Every wrong attempt discarded is another step forward.'

The map is not the territory: every person's map is unique
My way of looking at things is unique to me, yours unique to you. If you had chosen to write this book, you may have read all the same research material, and taken the same courses as me, yet the end result would have been very different. That is why there are so many reference books available on any given subject.

Think of the people with whom you are in contact at work – internally, colleagues, staff, senior managers; externally, customers and suppliers. How might their maps differ from yours? If you are able to put all the different perceptions together, you will come much closer to a complete picture than if you each stay within the boundaries of your own view. If you accept this NLP principle, then you respect and rejoice in difference.

Well-formed outcomes

Identifying and establishing *outcomes* is a central and first step in NLP. It's easy to say what you *don't* want. Focusing on an outcome you *do* want creates a much more engaging concept and gives you a clear indication of your commitment. If you don't make the choice for yourself in any aspect of your life then, by default, someone else will make it for you.

Creating well-formed outcomes

1 Positive
Every time you focus on what you can't do or don't want, you are creating a negative outcome and reminding yourself of what you want to avoid. How would you react if someone said to you: 'Don't look behind you!'? I know I would immediately turn my head. In order to avoid something, I have to think about it, and then to react to it. A much more useful instruction would be: 'Keep looking ahead.'

Divya, a manager in a busy customer-care office, agreed to reduce poor timekeeping in the office as part of her annual appraisal. This was a *negative and restrictive outcome*. When she decided to put a positive angle on it, she considered the question: 'What do I really want to happen?' She was then able to think about the real issue. Poor timekeeping meant the office was sometimes empty. An empty office led to the 'hotline' phone ringing continuously without being answered, meaning lost customers. What Divya wanted was to maintain existing customers and increase the number of new ones who joined the 'hotline' service. She was now able to think about changing conditions and creating flexible working patterns that would lead to at least one phone being operated all the time – *a more creative and outward-looking outcome*. She decided to introduce flexible rostering, particularly at 'twilight' and 'sunset' shifts.

2 Specific

Be specific in describing your positive outcome, and use as many questions as you can to check how specific you are. Moving from general to specific enables you to concentrate on answers and solutions.

Divya asked herself the following:

Where? – in the red office.

Who?   – I need at least one member of the team to be available for customer calls.

When? – from 0800 until 2200 hours.

> What? – I will arrange a change of working hours.
>
> How? – in individual and team discussions and meetings. We will review after the first three months.

3 Evidence

To enhance the energy and application of your outcome, it is useful to imagine as much sensory-based evidence as you can. This will increase your motivation too. If you don't know when you've achieved your outcome, you could still be using up resources long after you've actually succeeded.

> For Divya, this meant asking: what will I see, hear and feel, and how will others know this has been achieved?
>
> - I'll **see** at least one dedicated phone operator in the red room at all times.
> - I'll **hear** only three rings before the phone is answered.
> - I'll **feel** confident and relaxed about covering the lines.
> - They'll be able to **see** the roster every week, they'll **hear** words of encouragement from me and they'll **feel** acknowledged in their needs.

4 Ownership

Whose outcome is it? Be aware of whether you are dependent on someone else for your success. If you are waiting for others to change, you risk becoming a passive spectator. Consider your own part in and contribution to the process.

> Divya's key contribution is to identify what she wants, initiate discussion and, having agreed the procedures, to put these into practice.

5 Fit

How does the outcome fit in with other aspects of your life and your overall plan? Are there other people or factors to take into account? If you were to achieve your outcome, how would you feel about it? The response to this last question will indicate how important the outcome is.

> In terms of Divya's 'fit', knowing that customers' calls would be answered and that staff would be clearer about their responsibilities tied in with her being a constructive and collegiate manager. Other areas of the company would be positively affected by additional orders, and they would need to consider the additional administrative impact.

6 Resources

Sometimes, we forget that our resources are internal as well as external. A well-formed outcome will include consideration of both for initial achievement and then continued maintenance. If you accept that you have all the internal resources you need, the skill is to relate them specifically to your outcome. The acquisition of external resources may need greater planning. If you know what you need, you have a much better chance of designing the means of acquiring the requisite resources.

> Divya remembered the time she was on the receiving end of changes at work. She had felt involved and valued when Toby took the time to ask for her ideas and suggestions.She knew she had used his example to create an atmosphere of trust in her team, and felt confident of her ability to listen to their views.

Outcome checklist

Start with the questions below as you create your outcomes. It may be that as you go through the process, you find you are not meeting all the criteria. Keep amending them until you are happy. This is the linchpin of NLP and will give you the foundations you need for success.

Outcome checklist	
Positive	– what do you want? What would you like to happen?
Specific	– where, who, when, what and how?
Evidence	– what will you see, hear and feel when it is happening?
Ownership	– whose outcome is it, and what is your part in it?
Fit	– how much do you want it? How does it fit in with other aspects of your life?
Resources	– which have you used before and are transferable? Which do you need?

Summary

Today has provided an overview of Neuro-Linguistic Programming and covered the main principles which underpin NLP thinking. With well-formed outcomes, you can plan how you want to organise the rest of this NLP week. Tomorrow we will consider some individual and work-related principles and how to make them more empowering.

Personal and working beliefs

Yesterday we considered the basic principles that form NLP thinking. Today we will assess personal beliefs and how these affect you. In NLP it is paramount to start with yourself and understand what drives you to be the way you are before considering other people's styles and preferences.

From beliefs to action

What exactly do we mean when we talk about beliefs? In NLP terms, they represent the assumptions we make about ourselves, about others in the world and about how we expect things to be. These assumptions determine the way we behave and shape our decision-making processes. They are often based on emotions rather than facts. We tend to notice 'facts' that reinforce the beliefs. For example, if you believe that 'everyone is easy to get along with', you will only notice how well you interact with people. If, however, your belief is that 'you can't trust anyone', you will be suspicious and expect to be duped, and the chances are that others will sense this and be wary of you. Hence the term 'self-fulfilling prophecy': what you believe about yourself is what happens to you.

Samir's greatest challenge as a graduate manager was conducting performance reviews with older, more experienced staff. He had been brought up to **believe** that he **should** (a key word in beliefs) respect his elders and that they knew best. The young Samir took that to mean that he should not contradict or correct older (wiser) people. Stuck with that belief, how could he possibly discuss their underachievement? He knew all about preparation and setting objectives, it was just that every time he **thought** about one particular staff member, Riannon, he **felt** increasingly anxious. To make matters worse, she had once mentioned she was old enough to be his mother. He described what he **did** at her review: 'I decided to get straight to the point, and indicate where Riannon could make some improvements. Only I seemed to open my mouth and no words came out. She sat there smiling benignly and I told her everything was fine. I couldn't wait for it to be over.' Samir's underlying belief was limiting his ability to do his job effectively.

Begin to notice which beliefs drive your thoughts, feelings and actions. If your behaviour is not what you want and you think you can't change it, you have probably identified a limiting belief. If your beliefs are supportive and empowering, keep them. If they're restrictive, discard them. The rest of today will help do that.

Choices and changes

How do you know what to believe? You don't have to

dwell too much on the origin of your beliefs, but knowing
from whom or where they came can help you understand
what they mean to you. It can also lead you to a way to
change. We are generally given injunctions with the best
will in the world and for a very good reason at the time.
Trace back and identify the roots of what you believe about
yourself – notice where your beliefs originate. Can you hear
someone telling you to have that belief? Can you picture
being told, maybe more than once, or did you just sense
what was expected of you?

Remember Samir? He decided to revisit his original belief
and work out its meaning and relevance for him now. At
school he had always been a quick learner and could outwit
his parents in an argument. They felt intimidated and
concerned that he would be considered cheeky by his
teachers. Therefore they wanted him to accept the wisdom of
their experience without question – as a protective measure.
They also wanted him to progress at school with the teachers
on his side. As you can imagine this was not the way the
young Samir perceived it. Now he could start to think it
through and consider his choices: either to keep the limiting
belief and not question his older staff members, or to find a
more suitable and facilitating belief.

He decided that it was important for him to respect other
people and himself as equal and different human beings.
This was a present-day belief that he knew to be important
in all aspects of his life. His *feelings* about the next review
had changed to excited (and a little apprehensive), and he
thought about what he would say and how he would say it.
He reminded himself that 'There is no failure, only
feedback', and he *went* in search of Riannon to rearrange the

meeting, prepared to learn and develop.

It may well be that you have beliefs that you no longer need, and their purpose is obsolete. If that is so, then change them. Depending on their source this may seem quite challenging. Take your time to work through and understand their origin and intention. You can choose whatever you want to believe. Sometimes we choose, or have imposed on us, beliefs that are restrictive in nature. We bring them with us into all kinds of situations. Once we recognise them, we can choose to replace them or discard them completely. If you approach the question from the other side, you may be following the belief 'I have learnt many things in my life. Now is the time to update my repertoire.'

Whether you believe that 'NLP will work for me' or whether you believe 'it won't work for me', the chances are you will be proven right until you investigate the origin of the belief further. Your beliefs can work either with you and for you or despite you and against you.

NLP will work for me:

- 'I enjoy new ideas'
- 'I know I can change'
- 'I've learnt so much before, here's another opportunity'
- 'I've an open mind'

NLP won't work for me:

- 'You can't teach an old dog new tricks'
- 'I never pick up new ideas'
- 'I've tried things like this before – they never work'
- 'Nothing will make me change'

Which of your beliefs help or hinder you? Compulsive language which includes the words 'should', 'ought' or 'must' leads to patterns of behaviour that can become compulsive. If you have a belief that you want to change, you could ask:

- *Is this an empowering belief?*

- *Is this a limiting belief?*

- *Where has it come from?*

- *What was the positive intention behind it?*

- *How do I want to change it?*

Which of your beliefs would you like to change? Here's an example:

Belief	Empowering?	Restricting?	Source	Intention	Change
I must not make mistakes	No	Yes	School	Best performance	I can learn from my mistakes

Working beliefs

On Sunday, you considered the basic principles of NLP and imagined how it would be if they were yours. These were related to excellence and how it could be achieved. Today some additional principles, or beliefs, are set out that relate to the workplace:

We come to work to do our best

It is in everybody's interest that their work is as enjoyable and fulfilling as possible. Most people do the best they can given the system they are in. If you/your company can create the conditions for individuals to take responsibility and feel valued in their role, they will put their best into their job. If someone comes to work intent on sabotage, it may be that their needs are not being considered or that their beliefs are contrary to those of the company.

Our decisions are right at the time we make them
If this is your starting point, you are likely to be calmer and more understanding when you are reviewing performance with your staff. You do not have to accept their decision, just that it was right for them with the knowledge they had at the time. In fact, if you don't accept their decision, then take time to assess whether you have different or additional information that could help them reach another conclusion.

There may even be a chance that in the light of the ensuing discussion, you reconsider your position. If their decision has resulted in an error, remember to think in terms of feedback and learning.

Behind every action is a positive intention
Imagine how it might be if you had this amongst your working beliefs. It is not always clear why we continue with behaviours that are not apparently beneficial or make no sense to us. What makes us act in a way that sabotages our development? And if we do so, how does this belief make sense? We need to understand the intention and personal belief behind the action to understand it.

Ros was a manager who regularly complained of overwork and stayed back most nights to sort out her filing even though she had clerical assistants in her team. What was her positive intention behind this behaviour? Ros felt somewhat out of her depth in her existing role. She had always enjoyed general administration and knew this to be an area in which she was very competent. Her intention, therefore, was to boost her confidence in familiar routine. The effect, though, was to alienate her staff and give herself an unnecessary overload.

There are a number of answers to every question
This is the belief of flexibility and creativity. If you close your minds to allow only your own personal beliefs, then you close off many opportunities. If you are working as part of a team and are prepared to listen to all the ideas

available, then a more satisfactory outcome is likely to be found. Notice when you switch out other people's ideas. Does this happen with particular people, subject areas, times, places? Now imagine that these are useful ideas and that you want to incorporate them. This can open up a new way of behaving, thinking and believing.

Imagine that these working beliefs were your own working beliefs, and try them on for a period of time. Notice how they work for you. Write down their effect on you and your colleagues, and where you would like to apply them – for example, in an appraisal, discipline session, selection and recruitment, team meetings, negotiations.

Your colleagues may be surprised if your behaviour changes significantly. Stick with it, and over time you will reap the rewards.

Perceptual positions

One powerful way to increase your effectiveness in relating
to others is to extend your information about the way they
behave and how they make their choices. The NLP
technique called *perceptual positions* provides a practical
way to do this. On those occasions when you seem stuck in
your communication, it can be very valuable to change
your position (literally and figuratively) and take different
views of the situation. This is sometimes called *second
guessing*. If you can understand their thinking and work out
their positive intentions, then you have added knowledge
to take you forward.

The three basic perceptual positions

- 1st position: *self* – this is your own reality, how *you* see,
  hear and feel about the situation. You think
  and feel in terms of what matters to *you*.

- 2nd position: *other* – this is the other person's reality,
  how it would look, sound and feel if you
  were them. How might it affect them?

- 3rd position: *observer* – this is the detached observer.
  How might this situation appear to
  someone who is not involved? You can
  watch both parties interact and
  understand without experiencing either
  person's emotions.

Within companies, you can become so involved in
production or service delivery (1st position, *your* map) that
you may not know whether your efforts are being

channelled in the most productive way. Your many customers will have their own views about your service, and you may find it useful to gain insight into their map through the 2nd perceptual position. Ask yourself: 'What would I think about delivery times and quality if I were one of my customers?' The third, observer's position enables you to assess the interactions between 1 and 2 without any of the emotional interference. Imagine you were outside the situation. You could then ask: 'What does the relationship between Shmikes Ltd and its front-line customers seem like?'

When Hannah was asked to describe her role at work, she said she felt like 'piggy in the middle'. She had the top team complaining about the operatives and the shop stewards expecting her to sort out management. In 1st position, she was able to work out what she wanted from the situation, namely to gain clarity and stand her ground. From 2nd position, she studied the other views and beliefs that might be around. She concluded that both the top team and the shop stewards came to her because she was able to communicate equally and fairly. From their positions, Hannah was an objective onlooker who listened to their opinions with no vested interest. The more she considered their positions, the more she was able to see her role as constructive. In 3rd position, Hannah noticed that her sense of frustration was blocking her effectiveness and that it would be beneficial if she valued the trust they had in her and could maintain neutrality to help their cause. Piggy in the middle became a skilled mediator.

Practise perceptual positions for yourself and notice how they help the situation you choose.

Exercise

- Think of an unsatisfactory situation between you and someone else.
- Put three sheets of paper on the floor, labelled 'self', 'other' and 'observer'.
- Stand on the 'self' sheet, facing the 'other', and recognise how you experience the situation you have chosen. Know what you would like to say to the other person. Then move away and turn around.
- Stand on the 'other' sheet and imagine you are that person looking at the 'self'. Recognise how you, as the other person, might experience the interaction. What would you like to say to 'self'? Then move away and turn around.
- Step onto the 'observer' sheet and look at 'self' and 'other'. From this neutral position, notice what is happening. What is or isn't being achieved? Remember that you do not take sides: this is the place for objective assessment. If you notice any emotions as you stand on 'observer', check whether they belong to 'self' or 'other' and go back to that sheet. 'Observer' is a neutral position. Then move away and turn around.
- Move back to 'self' and repeat the stages as many times as you need to gain full information and insight.
- Decide what you will do as a result of your new understanding.

Perceptual positioning is also useful when you are considering launching a new product, have a proposal to make or are checking the 'fit' of an outcome. By thinking in the following terms, you will be able to broaden your approach and increase your flexibility:

- How might other staff feel about this approach?
- How will this look from the customers', suppliers', manufacturers' and employees' points of view?
- What would this sound like to the sales team?

Create some of your own questions to help you understand as many views as possible of any situation.

Summary

Today you have been able to clarify those beliefs that are empowering and have started to change or discard those that are limiting. Tomorrow you will discover the different ways that people process information.

Knowing yourself and others

Today we will concentrate on the clues and cues that help
you recognise your own and other people's preferred
thinking and communication styles. In NLP, these are called
accessing cues because they help you access the way
someone is processing whatever is happening around them.

When someone poses a question, or says something to you
in a conversation, you may need anything from a fraction
of a second to a couple of minutes to process your thoughts
and then respond. The way you do this has an important
effect on the way you communicate or miscommunicate
with others. In NLP, the term *'representational systems'* is
used to describe this processing of information.

Representational systems

We represent information internally through our basic
senses, i.e. in pictures (*visual*), sounds (*auditory*), feelings
(*kinaesthetic*), taste (*gustatory*) and smells (*olfactory*). The
words in brackets are the NLP terminology used to refer to
the senses. We all see, hear, feel, smell and taste in our own
way, unless we have some neurological damage.

As you **look** at this page in the book, you may be
distracted by the ringing of the telephone. As you **hear**
your HR manager's voice, you **feel** nervous and slightly
apprehensive, wondering about your recent promotion
interview. You **tell** yourself that if you are successful
you will go out for a meal at your favourite restaurant.
You may remember the last time you ate there, the
smell of the herbs and spices and the **taste** of the ...
as you took your first mouthful ...

Be aware of how many of your senses you used to follow
the above passage. You may have found it easier to picture
people or places as you read. You may have been more
comfortable recreating sounds or noticing sensations and
feelings. The senses of smell and taste may have made you
salivate, distracting you even more. What you were doing
was using your internal senses to *represent* the external
experiences described through the words.

Different people will have different responses. None is right
or wrong, they just are. It is important to remember that
these comprise information and are not a way of

stereotyping people. The skill is to recognise, without judging, the systems being used and to work with them. Excellent communicators do this instinctively. They move around the *representational systems* to include and reach each member of their audience. In any presentation, they will use all the three main representational systems (visual, auditory and kinaesthetic) to be sure that everyone can either see, hear or make sense of the points they are making. In the same way as our map of the world only represents part of the territory, so our preferred representational system is only part of the picture, or is only one sound bite, or feels incomplete.

Predicates

Predicates are the words we use that differentiate between representational systems. In visual mode, Sasha would like to **see** the minutes of a meeting **written** down for her to **read**. In auditory, Denise would prefer to **hear** what happened or **talk** it over with someone else, particularly the section that wasn't on her **wavelength**. If Phil wanted to **touch** base after the meeting to **weigh up** his and others' **sense** of the meeting, he would be in kinaesthetic mode. These three could have a frustrating post-meeting discussion if they became stuck in their own preferred system.

Over time, we develop preferences for one of the representational systems, and will tend to use that more often. Although, in different contexts, we may well use the other systems too, it is just that we become more comfortable and practised in one of the three. In any discussion where different systems are being used exclusively, an interpreter may be needed.

Which is your preferred system? Think back to your last meeting or team briefing and write down or tape-record the words to describe it, or draw a diagram. What were the first words that came into your head? Now consider your last customer meeting, with internal or external customers, and repeat the process. Finally, think about your most recent experience of moving house and write or tape the words. Did you find your preferred system?

There was probably a strong secondary system and a weaker third. Now listen to and note your colleague's words. When you recognise their preferred systems, you may understand them better. Are you speaking the same language? You may well find that these change depending on the context. Notice what happens and extend your knowledge of yourself and others.

Predicate identifier examples

Visual	Auditory	Kinaesthetic	Olfactory/ gustatory
Looks good to me	Sounds right	Feels good	Fresh as a daisy
Outside my picture	Can't hear myself think	Heated debate	Smell a rat
Seeing eye to eye	Singing our tune	On common ground	A sweet person
Shed some light on...	Clear explanation	Hands on	Get the flavour ...
Colourful show	Rings bells ...	Smooth operator	Whiff of success

Eye movements

You can also gain further information about representational systems via the eye-accessing cues which concentrate on eye movements. Research in NLP suggests that people using the visual representational system tend to look upwards or ahead, while those using auditory look sideways and those using kinaesthetic look downwards. Further refinement indicates that, in general, a right-handed person looks up to their left when they are recalling past experiences and up to their right when they are creating an image for the first time. For some left-handed people, the patterns are reversed. As this is a generalised model, check your observations in as many ways as you can, using *calibration* – which appears later today – as a way of observing each person's unique cues.

As you go through the following exercises, you may find that you respond differently from the suggested eye movements. Don't despair: you're not wrong or strangely built; work out your individual patterns.

Visual

A person using visual accessing cues will answer the questions below after locating a picture in their mind. Invite someone to ask you these questions and to note where your eyes go. Then swap round with them and note their eye movements. You don't need to speak the answers. What matters is *how* you arrive at them. Analysing eye movements takes practice, and over time you will notice patterns with ease.

> What did your first work space look like? *(Your eyes up and to your left.)*
>
> Imagine your MD with pink hair and wearing a bright orange suit? *(Your eyes up and to your right.)*

A person with a preferred visual representational system will want to see diagrams and charts and be more likely to use flip charts or overhead projectors. They may need to see things in writing and prefer electronic mail to telephone calls.

Auditory

When people are thinking in sounds, their eyes move across to their left for remembered sounds and to their right for imagined sounds.

> Recite your 2 times table. (*Your eyes across to your left.*)
>
> How would your voice sound underwater? (*Your eyes across to your right.*)

Those with a preferred auditory representational system will want to discuss issues. They like to talk and often 'think out loud' as they gather their thoughts for themselves. They tend to prefer the phone to electronic mail.

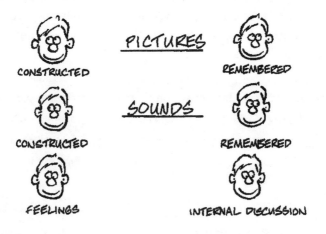

Fig 1: *Typical eye-accessing cues for right-handed people as you look at them*

Kinaesthetic
If someone's eyes look down and to their right, they are processing in kinaesthetic mode, and this puts them in touch with either their internal emotions or an external tactile feeling. They may also be in olfactory or gustatory mode.

How do you react when you
are angry?

How would you feel in
sinking sand?

Think of your favourite scent.

What does ice cream taste like?

*(Your eyes down
and to your right.)*

Kinaesthetics will start with their 'gut feelings' in the way
they react to different situations. They will want to work
out how they feel about an issue – they 'just have a sense'
about things. They pick up underlying and unspoken
feelings.

Internal dialogue
When people are in conversation with themselves, having
an 'internal dialogue', then their eyes will tend to look
down and to their left. This is another system of thinking,
and it can take longer to process before responding. It is
often associated with people being 'deep in thought'. The
key to communicating with a person using this mode is to
give them plenty of time. They can become confused or
frustrated if you keep asking supplementary questions
through your impatience.

In quiet times, what do you
find yourself thinking about?

Repeat silently: 'I am who
I am and I am fine.'

*(Your eyes down
and to your left.)*

QUICK, HIGH PITCH

CLEAR, RESONANT

DEEP, SLOW

VISUAL   AUDITORY   KINAESTHETIC

Please note that these are generalisations only. Not everyone fits neatly into them. What you may notice is that although someone's eyes move in an unexpected direction, they are likely to be consistent so you can learn to recognise their system. Remember to notice their predicates too for confirmation.

Body language

The gestures you make, the qualities in your voice and the way you breathe are further indicators of the representational system being used at any time. These may be the first aspects you notice or the final check after you have heard the predicates and detected the eye movements.

	Visual	Auditory	Kinaesthetic
Voice	Speak quickly and in a higher pitch than A or K.	Clear, expressive, rich and resonant.	Deeper, slower, with pauses.
Head	Head up, shoulder muscles tense.	Well-balanced or leaning to one side.	Angled downwards.
Breath	Centred high in chest area and shallow.	Evenly over whole chest area.	Deep and low in abdomen.
Gestures	Exaggerated. Sit/ stand erect. Gestures upwards.	Move rhythmically. Touching ears or near ears. Lips move.	Relaxed posture, with rounded shoulders.

Calibration

Where eye movements and body language give you a generalised overview of representational systems, *calibration* involves recognising and applying the different information that is unique to each person. How is this useful at work? As you become increasingly aware of the individual and minimal cues from a person, you will be able to recognise a pattern from which to assess their mood. You will also be able to evaluate the effect you are having without just relying on the words.

There are many cues to notice. Some you will already spot subconsciously and just know what someone is going to do or say before they do or say it. Notice the information available from someone's breathing, muscle tone or skin colour.

Rapport

If your communications always seem to be successful and without conflict, well done. It would seem that you are using all the information available and then adapting your representational style to suit the person with whom you are communicating. This is known in NLP terminology as *being in rapport*.

Rapport is the process of building and sustaining a relationship of mutual trust, harmony and understanding. This happens through matching the accessing cues from words, eye movements and body language.

Rapport enables you to appreciate the other person's map of the world. If you make the effort to be like someone else, they will feel more comfortable in their dealings with you. They are more likely to trust you and do business with you. People tend to like people who are like them. There is a Native American proverb: 'Let me not judge my neighbour until I have walked a mile in his moccasins', which is a lovely description of rapport. You could also demonstrate rapport by seeing things from someone else's point of view, playing the same tune or getting under their skin in a positive way.

Matching

Rapport is partly established by *matching* the representational systems and body language of others. This might mean sitting down if they are seated, breathing slowly like them or speaking at a fast pace with them. They will have the sense that you are 'with and for' them rather than against them. The advantage of matching is that the other person recognises at an unconscious level that you understand and value what they are communicating. It will also help you unconsciously to join in genuinely with their understanding.

> Margaret wanted to practise her matching skills. She had been invited to attend a client briefing with a training organisation, OT Training, for whom she was the newest associate. She noticed that the client was primarily using an auditory language pattern and sat with his chin cupped in his hands. He also spoke slowly and at an even pace. When Margaret spoke, she matched the rhythm. Whenever he changed his posture, she followed unobtrusively. She enjoyed the meeting. Even more so when OT's director rang to tell her that they had gained the contract on the proviso that Margaret was lead trainer.

It is worth noting that you can disagree with someone and still be in rapport: you are disagreeing from as close as you can be to their map of the world. You can also agree wholeheartedly with someone and not be in rapport because you are not 'speaking' the same language. With practice, matching can be performed elegantly and without detection. It is equally important that you match with integrity, not as a cynical means of tricking someone to your advantage.

Mismatching
There may be occasions when you no longer wish to be involved in a discussion or want to switch the focus. Imagine what would happen if you deliberately *mismatched* the other person(s) involved. In most cases, they will respond and move away or change direction. An extreme form of mismatching is turning your back.

Pacing and leading

Pacing extends rapport by respecting and responding to someone's emotional state. When we talk about a person's excitement or enthusiasm being 'infectious', we are merely describing our ability to pace and join in with them. You know what it is like if you go into work full of joy on a Monday morning: if colleagues pace your mood, you continue to feel good. If they say: 'It's all right for some' or 'Don't know why you're so cheerful. Wait till you see your in-tray', you may feel deflated.

If you can match and pace someone's mood, then you can lead them away from it too. So, for example, if someone is becoming increasingly angry at a meeting, you can help them calm down without 'losing face'. Alternatively, in an appraisal meeting, it would be helpful to understand and acknowledge the other person's nerves before creating a more conducive climate. The general rule is to pace a couple of times to make sure you have understood before *leading* to change. If you start to lead too soon, it will just seem like a mismatch and you will lose the rapport.

A travel organisation wanted to restructure its customer care programme. It called in an NLP expert who introduced a series of ideas including pacing and leading. Staff were most challenged by those irate, often anxious, customers who thought they had been let down by the organisation, the main concern being delays and overlong travel times. They practised pacing the 'customer' by matching the energy of the mood and emotions displayed. For example, they talked more quickly, in staccato phrasing and with a sense of urgency. After a couple of exchanges, they lowered their voice, and slowed their pace and breathing. They had moved to a more resourceful state and started to *lead* to solutions and options. They were overjoyed when their customers followed and calmed down too. Both parties had wanted a positive outcome. It was just that they had started from initially incompatible places.

Impact at work

Introducing change in the workplace is more acceptable if you can first match and pace the parties involved. Some basic research about how best to manage information saves time and conflict later on. People like and feel understood by people who are like themselves. So consider: would your colleagues want to see a written account of your proposals, would they rather talk them over, or would they prefer time to grasp and sense the nature of your ideas?

Think how you might approach the situations shown using each of the three main representational systems. Write or record a prepared statement for each following the example shown.

	Visual	Auditory	Kinaesthetic
Recruitment interview	We've looked at your CV. Where do you see yourself in 5 years?	It sounds like you have wide expertise. Tell me about …	In which of your last jobs did you feel most settled?
Closing a meeting			
Staff briefing			
Appraisal			
Customer meeting			

Summary

The way people process information is crucial to communications both at work and outside. Learning to recognise and understand this, you can increase your success in communications. Practise rapport and notice others who seem to do it naturally. What do they do and what can you learn from them?

Tomorrow you will have the chance to develop a set of precision questions to ensure you understand someone else's message.

What exactly do you mean?

Yesterday you worked out both someone's preferred way of accessing information and how to establish rapport. However, there may still be areas of misunderstanding. This is because the meaning of the words you use can be more complicated than they sound. You know what *you* want to say, and *you* know what the words mean. The challenge arises when you are speaking in your own 'shorthand', expecting the message to be understood, even acted upon, by someone else. It is unfortunate if, as far as the other party is concerned, you have only given out half the 'story', or one that has different interpretations. Words don't always relate the intended meaning because the audience will interpret them in their own way.

Meta model

For those occasions when you want to know clearly and specifically what the words mean, you can use the NLP process known as the *meta model*.

Meta model – a series of devices for achieving a better understanding of vague language patterns, including specific questions for added clarification.

There are times both at work and outside when it is crucial that we are clear and precise in what we say. If you are the health and safety officer who states that: 'There mustn't be too many people at this gathering because of the fire risk', that won't do. Equally, if you are talking in terms of a multi-million-pound deal and you suggest a profit share of 'around 10%ish', or in an appraisal meeting you say 'You're always out of touch with the rest of the section', you are not providing information in a form to which others can make a valid response. This is a case not of your being deliberately awkward but of your just missing out some information that you assume they know. At other times, it is fine to be imprecise because we are with someone who understands our shorthand or we want to encourage creativity.

Linguistic research suggests that there is a difference between 'deep' and 'surface' structure levels of language. Deep structure describes the complete and whole experience you go through subconsciously before saying the words to convey your message. Surface structure represents the words you speak both internally to yourself (your own personal shorthand) and audibly to others. It is the conscious representation of your deep structure. If you put all your deep-structure thinking into words, the most basic narrative would take so long that you would lose your audience. Between deep structure and surface structure, we delete, distort and generalise our experience and verbalise the representation.

The meta model provides the techniques to enable you to recover information from another person which they have deleted, distorted or generalised en route from their deep structure. This avoids you wondering if you have guessed right. You can fill in the gaps and reconnect to the fuller meaning. When you are wondering 'Why are you saying this?', 'What exactly are you trying to tell me?' or 'What do you want me to do?', the meta model provides a set of more elegant questions to help you find out. If we don't ask the questions, we may find we have moved a long way down conflicting paths because of an unnecessary misunderstanding.

Deletions
We delete all kinds of information when we presume that the other person will know what we mean, or when we consider it too trivial to include. The following are the most common deletions:

Unspecified nouns
In this pattern, you describe an action without clarifying *who* carried it out. This is sometimes used when the speaker wants to express their dissatisfaction and to avoid conflict by not naming names. It also depersonalises situations where the speaker seems to be a passive bystander – so taking no responsibility for what is happening.

- 'He's not liked'
- 'They don't tell you anything'
- 'It's so difficult'

- 'Who specifically doesn't like him?'
- 'Who exactly?
- 'What precisely is so difficult?'

Unspecified verbs

In this pattern, you describe an action without clarifying *how* it was carried out. You may want to understand the behaviour behind a particular action, and you need to know *how* something was done.

- 'We will be the most efficient ... '
    'How exactly will we be the most efficient?'
- 'She's avoiding me'
    'How specifically is she avoiding you?'

Nominalisation

'Any *communication* which includes lengthy *discussions* in an *organisation* is likely to lead to *confusion*!' What on earth did you take that sentence to mean? It is full of *nominalisations*. The word 'nominalisation' is used to describe what happens when we take a verb or process which is dynamic and change it into a noun so that it becomes static. (These are also referred to as *abstract nouns*.) Meta-model questions enable you to find out the processes or actions that are missing.

- Any communication   'How do you communicate?'
- Lengthy discussions   'What are you discussing?'
- Organisation   'What are you organising?'
- Confusion   'How are you confusing yourself?'

Nominalisations are common in business and politics. They are often deliberately vague and abstract, meaning any number of different things to different people. Nominalisations become a challenge when they are mistaken for reality and you think they actually exist. Nominalisations delete so much information that we take the empty shell and fill it with our own ideas and assumptions. Compare 'raising the stakes' with 'development in investments'. The first describes an active process while the second is static and implies no active participation.

Nominalisations can be recognised when the noun makes sense with the word 'ongoing' in front of it. An ongoing

relationship or ongoing enterprise will probably relate to an abstract noun, while an ongoing dog won't. The other test is whether or not 'it' will fit into a wheelbarrow. You would struggle to put development or training into a wheelbarrow, whereas several cats would probably fit quite comfortably.

Comparisons
Sometimes, we can make a statement that implies a comparison but is unclear as to what we are comparing. Our listener, rather than assuming, will want to know the rest of the information.

- ' … resulting in greater customer loyalty'
  'Greater compared to what?'
- 'She's better at organising'
  'Better than whom?'

Judgements
'It is a truth universally acknowledged, that a single man in possession of a good fortune, must be in want of a wife.' (Jane Austen, *Pride and Prejudice*.) If this were spoken, rather than the opening lines of a novel, you might be inclined to reply: 'Says who?' Yet when people make these kinds of global statements, they can be very powerful and are often received without question. The speaker is deleting the fact that this is an opinion and expressing their beliefs as if they were an absolute fact. They are presenting their map of the world as the only one. In addition, they do not identify who is making the judgement. It may be important for you to know the source of the judgement before deciding your response. It can also help the other person to consider 'Who said this in the first instance?' and 'Is it still relevant or useful for me now?'

- 'That is the way to do it'   'According to whom?'
- 'His incompetence is worrying'
  'Who thinks he is incompetent?'

Distortions

Distortions occur when a speaker draws conclusions that have no logical foundation, or assumes faulty connections between different parts of their experience. The skill is to discover what evidence you or the other person has to suggest that their distortion is fact.

Mind reading

These are the kind of interpretations people make when they presume that they know what someone else is thinking or feeling. It is important to check whether this intuitive response to someone is accurate or whether it could be affecting a relationship on the basis of guesswork.

- 'He's ignoring me'   'How do you know?'
- 'I'm sure she loves surprises'   'How can you be sure?'

You can also turn this mind reading around so that you give another person the power to read your mind. They then become responsible for your well-being or otherwise and can be blamed for not understanding you. The classic 'You'd know if you really loved me' is a typical example of this. The meta-model question in response would be: 'How would I know?'

Complex equivalent
This often follows mind reading because it links two statements as if they have the same meaning – e.g. 'You are frowning, and that means I'm in trouble.' Here, frowning is equated with being in trouble, which is not necessarily the case: some people frown when they are concentrating. The question for this pattern is: 'How does this mean that?'

- 'He's ignoring me'   'How do you know?'
- 'He didn't wave back when   'How does his not waving
  I drove past this morning.   mean he is ignoring you?'
  He must be ignoring me'

Cause and effect
This pattern involves one thing having a causal relationship with another. Rather than the complex equivalent assuming that x means y, here the distortion is that x causes y and there is some sequence to the events. Use of the word 'but' is sometimes a clue to this pattern.

- 'I was going to say something but knew it would ruin things'   'How would saying something ruin things?'
- 'Involving the top team will lead to solvency'   'How will involving the top team cause us to become solvent?'

Presuppositions

These do exactly that and presuppose an underlying assumption about our beliefs and expectations. The classic question 'When did you stop beating your wife?' presupposes that beatings have happened and have now stopped. Whatever your answer, you are in a no-win situation. The responses to presuppositions are likely to include: 'What makes you think ...?', 'What leads you to believe ...?', or 'How do you know ...?'

'When you go to the meeting, are you voting for or against?' (This presupposes that you are going to the meeting and have decided which way to vote.) A useful response would be: 'What makes you think I am going? How do you know I'm voting?'

Generalisations

Generalisations involve interpreting one experience as an absolute truth which applies in all circumstances. They also describe the rules or limits which govern our behaviour.

When these are operating as part of our beliefs, we can seem to be dogmatic and rigid in discussions. Often, there is an element of fear attached to the very idea of being able to change or release these strongly held views.

Universal quantifiers
The language of universal quantifiers is likely to include such words as 'always', 'every', 'never', 'no-one', 'everyone', 'all' or 'nothing'. These words are all-inclusive and allow no room for manoeuvre. The meta model helps the speaker to recognise that their statement is not necessarily based on reality. They can then begin to expand and change their perceptions. One response you can make is to repeat back the key words with emphasis and then exaggerate to show how inane it is:

> • 'I'm always the last to know' 'Always? You're right of course. Everyone else in the business world knows before you'

Take care how you use this or you may not get the outcome you want.

Another way of responding is to check for a counter-argument:

> • 'Managers don't care about staff' 'Has there been a time when they did?'

Modal operators of necessity

These relate to the conditions and rules by which we run our lives. They implicitly seem to call on an unseen authority or unwritten rules, often originating in childhood. Modal operators of necessity are indicated by words like 'should', 'ought', 'must' and 'have to' or their negative equivalents. These are all words which externalise responsibility. By asking the question, 'What would happen if you did not do this?', you elicit the consequences of breaking the potentially constraining rule. This in turn enables the speaker to evaluate the present relevance of this rule.

- 'I must be available for work'   'What would happen if you weren't?'
- 'I shouldn't speak to strangers'   'What would happen if you did?'

Modal operators of possibility/impossibility

When a person says 'I can't' or 'It's impossible', they are talking about something that they perceive to be outside their ability or sphere of influence. In fact, it might just be their perception which is limiting them, not their ability or their situation. If this pattern goes unchecked, it can impair personal development as well as interpersonal relating.

Whenever you find yourself saying 'I can't' or 'I'll never manage that', check whether it is more a case of 'I won't', 'I haven't learned yet' or 'I don't want to'. You can instantly broaden your possibilities. You might also ask yourself: 'What's stopping me?' This will give you many insights into your map of the world.

As with the operators of necessity, you can also ask the question: 'What would happen if I did?' This is a very powerful question, and it can empower people to go beyond the barriers they build for themselves.

• 'I can't manage'	'What would happen if you could?'

This statement suggests that the person has some notion of managing – or how else do they know they are not doing it? As they consider what would happen if they *could* manage, they imagine possibilities and shift their thinking.

Summary

The meta model provides an invaluable set of precision questions for those occasions when you need or desire to be absolutely clear in your own mind as to what exactly someone is saying to you. Begin to notice any deletions, distortions and generalisations in your own internal dialogue.

Warning: this model can seem either an aggressive technique or overly pedantic. As with all NLP techniques the aim is to be elegant and appropriate in its use. It is essential to first create rapport, then your questions will be recognised as a constructive way of extending your understanding. Take some time to practise the questions in your own way, so that they sound natural. The ones used today are guidelines.

Filter systems

Today gives you the chance to understand how you respond to information you are given and how you programme it.

If you won a large amount of money tomorrow or were made redundant with a healthy severance package, what changes would it make to your life? Would your answers relate to all the things you could do – sail around the world, set up your own business, write a novel – or to all those things you wouldn't need to do anymore – stop worrying about bills, not have to go to work, not be cautious when shopping? The way you respond to this and any other questions will give you an idea about the way you filter experiences and information. In NLP, these filter systems are called *metaprograms*, and they are another way of explaining differences and misunderstandings in communication.

Metaprograms are the internal filters which people use to sort the information they receive in a systematic way, and which then determine their behaviour.

Metaprogram filters

It is important to recognise the flexibility that people have in the way they filter or sort their experiences. We habitually notice some experiences and screen out others, which leads to consistent patterns in the way we think and work.

PATTERNS OF BEHAVIOUR

The reason for identifying someone's metaprogram is to appreciate and understand differences. Once recognised, you can work with them from a position of rapport rather than conflict. The implications at work are immense: rather than being frustrated by someone else's 'pig headed' disagreements with you, once you can identify their metaprograms you can adapt your interaction to compensate. You may find you understand them better too.

Towards/away from

An example of a question to help determine this metaprogram is: 'If you took voluntary severance tomorrow, what changes would it make to your life?'

The example given at the start of today is a good indicator of whether you move *towards* your goals or *away from* unpleasant consequences. A towards person talks about benefits and knows what they want. An away-from person talks about problems and is more focused on what to avoid than on what to aim for. At work, a towards person will be a risk-taker and will have a 'go for it' approach. They may need an away-from person to anticipate possible pitfalls. An away-from person will put off doing something until the last minute, or until the disadvantages of not doing it become great enough to spur them on. Sometimes, they respond better to threats than to rewards. They may need a towards person to give them a push start.

Sameness/difference

An example of a question to help determine this metaprogram is: 'What is the relationship between the work you are doing now and the work you did last year?'

The answer to this question gives you an indication of whether a person considers information to find similarities and familiarity – 'still looking at' … 'the same as before' – or whether they do so to find difference and exception – 'changed projects', 'new clients with a different slant'. A person who prefers *sameness* will probably be happy to stay in the same or similar type of job and not look for changes. They can often find areas of mutuality. A *difference* person, on the other hand, wants variety at work and is more likely to make a number of career changes. The latter are often the rule breakers.

In addition, there are people whose attention is focused primarily on sameness, with secondary emphasis on the differences, or people who sort for the difference first before considering the similarities. Together, they form a large enough proportion of the population to be the main target for many advertisers. They will reject 'new' unless it is an improved version of the existing model, or 'improved' unless it still has some of the original qualities. What could be better than the familiar with some extra spice?

Internal/external

An example of a question to help determine this metaprogram is: 'How do you know when you have done a good job?'

This is sometimes called the *frame of reference* filter because it refers to the way people make judgements about their actions. An *internally* referenced person would be likely to answer the above question with words like 'I just know' or 'I feel good inside.' On the other hand, the responses 'When someone tells me' or 'When people use my ideas' both represent an *externally* referenced person. Internals are self-motivating people who want to make their own decisions. They work best with minimal supervision which recognises their preference to think for themselves. Externals want someone else to set the standards against which to assess themselves. They like to receive clear, positive feedback, and appreciate accessible management.

General/detail

An example of a question to help determine this metaprogram is: 'Tell me about the last film you saw.'

A *general* person would probably give you a broad overview and describe the film as 'a comedy, sci-fi film with excellent special effects', whereas a *detail* person might tell you about the different characters, the subplots, the music and the costumes. A general person thinks about the big picture and overall concepts. They will often leave out the 'small print' and encourage you to 'get to the point'. Their detail counterpart likes to deal with small pieces of data and works well with 'step by step' information. They often assess a situation in terms of all the pieces that make up the whole.

The members of a small amateur dramatics company were all losing patience with one of the actors. She insisted that when the table was laid, the spoons and plates must be in the same place every time, and that someone kept moving them. Operating from a detail perspective she needed to know that the table was set correctly. The producer calmed her down by suggesting that the really important thing was to have the correct number of everything on the table, and that the other actors could use their dramatic abilities to move things around.

This may seem trivial, but it changed a potential lynching into a smoother-running production.

Options/procedures

An example of a question to help determine this metaprogram is: 'Why did you choose your last job?'

Options people would give reasons for their choice like: 'The terms and conditions suited me', 'They gave me scope to develop my own style.' A *procedures* person would more likely describe *how* they chose, e.g.: 'I bought all the relevant trade journals, selected vacancies in the areas I would move to … ', thus giving you the procedure they followed. Options people may follow a procedure to begin with and then add variations to suit. They are motivated in a setting where they have freedom of choice to expand the possibilities available to them. The procedures person likes to follow the set task sequence and enjoys doing things to meet the 'standard'. They like a clearly defined course of action and detailed instructions.

Proactive/reactive

An example of a question to help determine this metaprogram is: 'How do you take the initiative?'

Proactive people take the initiative by getting on with things at their own prompting. They are self-starters who shoot first and ask questions later. *Reactive* people wait and respond to others who ask for help. They are good at analysing tasks and gathering information before taking action. Proactive people can make mistakes by ignoring the analysis and planning stages in decision-making. Reactive people may slow things down by too much analysis or because they are waiting for someone else to take responsibility.

The table shown gives an overview of the different metaprograms covered so far. The language column briefly describes the words associated with each. The work pattern/role column indicates the areas and types of work that would be suitable for people with those metaprograms. The final column, 'Response', suggests the words you might use to establish rapport with each.

Metaprograms	Language	Work pattern/role	Response
Towards	Get, have, gain, attain, achieve	Sales, innovation	Goal-oriented, incentives
Away from	Avoid, steer clear, exclude, prevent	Problem-solving, auditing	Point out dangers of not doing
Same	Usual, familiar, always, similar	Mediation, trends, negotiation	In common, traditional
Difference	New, change, one-off, different	Marketing, consultancy	Unique, special, revolutionary
Internal reference	I decide, I made the decision …	Self-employed, MD	Only you can decide/will know
External reference	What do you think? Is that OK?	Team players, certificates	Others think, the facts show
General	Overall, big picture, globally	Explorer	Basically, framework
Detail	Specifically, precisely	Pilot, architect	Structure, exactly, Let's be clear
Options	Choice, possibility	Teachers	Brainstorm, variety
Procedure	Necessity, must	Filing, accounts	Known way, proven
Proactive	Initiative, action, future plans	Personal assistant, troubleshooters	Independent, direct
Reactive	Respond, reaction, past achievement	Help desk, receptionist	Analysis, waiting

You may want to consider the different combinations and how they work together. You may find you are mainly a towards person who is externally referenced and proactive.

Does that suit the job you do? It is worth remembering that your metaprograms are likely to be contextual.

Company metaprograms
It is possible that the company you work in or the managers and staff you work with have similar metaprograms to yourself. However, if you feel like an outsider, this may suggest that your metaprograms are different in significant ways. It can be very frustrating if you are proactive and your employers are reactive, using crisis management as their norm. Your company may be externally referenced, wanting to know what is going on and what can be learned throughout the industry, rather than just being committed to excellence from within.

Different departments will need different metaprograms: options people who mismatch will work well in research and development, while detail and procedures people will create an efficient finance section. Teams that have a balance of metaprograms amongst their members will be more effective.

Sorting categories
Think about your first day at work. The elements you remember will depend on the sorting categories you use. Knowing that none is right or wrong, recognise the way you sort information.

First-day memories might focus on:

• People	– the person who showed you around, your immediate manager, your team members, new friends
• Places	– the location, your office, the restaurant, the main reception area

- Things   – your desk, chair, computer, paintings, coffee-making facilities
- Activity   – induction, team meeting, staff briefing, phone calls
- Time   – when it happened, dates, what you did hour by hour
- Information – how you chose the job, why you joined the company

It is very useful to recognise another person's focus of interest in a particular context. Being people-focused is important for staff at the customer interface as they will respond better to the customer's needs. An activity focus will be helpful to someone who is organising the weekly rotas.

Which focus is important in your job? Which is your favourite sorting category?

Time travel

The way we relate to time also has implications for the way we communicate. Some people seem to live in the past, remembering the way things were. They might talk about how things were done in their last job. Others live for now and their attention is on the present moment. They talk about the here and now and 'Let's do it.' Future-oriented people tend to plan and to be thinking about the future. They are the sort of people who want to know what they will be having for tea just as they finish their lunch. Consider which way you and those around you relate to time. What could you change to take you closer to them? There are benefits to any team if you have all three of the above types available as long as they appreciate each other's value to the team.

Timelines

People code time in different ways. We may use the same
words, 'past', 'present', 'future', but we will place them
differently in the way we represent them in our minds.
How do you know whether something is a past memory or
a plan for the future? In NLP, the term *timeline* is used to
explain where people position their concepts of time.

Find your timeline:

- Think about four events from your past. Where
  were those memories positioned? If you were to
  point to their location, would they be behind you,
  in front, to the left or to the right of you?
- As you read this book now, decide where now is.
  Point to indicate: is it inside you, in front of you, or
  to the left or right of you?
- Now think about three probable events from your
  future, starting with next week and going as far
  ahead as you wish. Where were those thoughts
  positioned? Point to their location and notice from
  which direction they came.

This will give you an idea of where you place time, and
if you were to plot and join up the dots, you could trace
the direction of your line.

In time

The timeline known as 'in time' is so called because in this
representation a person has time passing through them:
their past is behind them, their future is ahead of them and
their present is inside them. They are *in* their timeline.

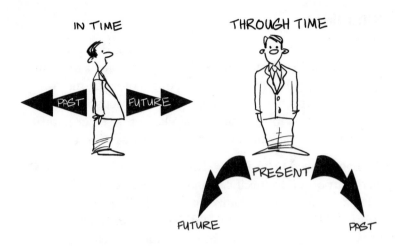

Fig 2: *Through-time and in-time timelines*

These people tend to concentrate on the present and may be less good at planning and setting deadlines. Their idea of 'urgent' may be quite flexible because they do not strongly connect what they are doing now with what will happen in the future. They can tend to be late because they are so involved in now and easily lose track of time.

Through time
When someone is operating on a 'through time' timeline, they have their past, present and future in front of them. They think of events as a series of related episodes, where time is linear, continuous and uninterrupted. It is likely that through-time people are the designers of time-management schemes, and cannot comprehend how they might be unclear to in-time people. Through-time people tend to arrive on time and place a high value on punctuality. They are also excellent at forward planning.

Chunking

We manage information at different levels and in different-sized *chunks*. You can change the way someone is thinking about an issue by *chunking up* – taking a broader, more general perspective – or *chunking down* – discussing a set of tasks necessary for the success of a key project – or *chunking sideways* – into a related or comparative area of research.

Managers need to be able to chunk down high-level projects and purposes into specific, manageable and delegated tasks. They will also have to chunk up the collective goals of their individual staff to form unit and departmental plans. The concept of diversification represents sideways chunking.

Summary

Warning: time lines and metaprograms are generalisations of how people process information and of their resultant behaviour. They are not absolutes, and they will alter with the context. They are not right or wrong, just different. As with all NLP concepts, their purpose is to enable you to think about patterns that help you to understand and communicate better.

Levels of change and reframing

We have already considered how our representational systems, language and thinking patterns can explain some of the differences in the way we communicate and process information. Today, we will extend that thinking beyond these different perspectives to the different levels of experience that influence the way we live our lives. We will also review a specific NLP technique, *reframing*, as another way to enable change.

Neuro logical levels of change

One of NLP's leading thinkers, Robert Dilts, suggests that there are six levels of learning, communication and change. He terms these *neuro logical levels* because they fit together in a logical, hierarchical way.

From the highest level to the lowest:

- Spirituality/purpose – who else?
- Identity/mission – who?
- Belief systems and values – why?
- Capabilities – how?
- Behaviour – what?
- Environment – where?

Dilts suggests that any changes made at the higher levels will have a greater influence on you than those made at the lower levels. The most important factor for effective change is to recognise the level at which you are stuck in any particular context. Once you can do that for yourself, you will be able to understand and match other people's levels too. The neuro logical levels are also relevant to companies.

> When the directors of Markys introduced an appraisal system across the board, they encountered fierce opposition from their first-line supervisors. This imposed change at the behaviour level did not fit in with the supervisors' views at the identity level: 'We're not managers' was their first response, followed by a capabilities concern: 'We're not trained to do this.' A little research and discussions with the supervisors would have saved Markys from the struggle it endured.

Neuro logical levels can help you develop greater flexibility in the way you think about all aspects of your life. If you seem to be in an unsatisfactory situation of any kind, you may find that applying neuro-logical-level questions helps you to locate and alter the source of your unease. You can use the levels to extend your awareness of what in your life is working for you. The descriptions below explain each neuro logical level and then offer some applications for individuals and in companies.

Connectedness/purpose
This level refers to the larger system of which you are a part. In a metaphysical sense, it involves understanding your purpose in whatever you do in the world around you. This is *your* innermost sense of yourself, and it is sometimes called your 'higher purpose'. This level gives you a sense of whether or not you are fulfilled in what you are doing. If

your feelings are strong at this level, you may only need to make minor adjustments elsewhere. If this is where you feel unease, then you might need to make changes across the board.

At this level, you would be answering the question: 'Why am I here?'

- *Individual implications:* 'No man is an island', and so whatever changes you make in your life are likely to affect those around you and will include a consideration of your higher purpose. Your decisions about the type of work you would prefer to do will be influenced by the systems to which you want to belong. Given the choice, most people work in settings that complement their ethical position, otherwise they can find themselves at odds with the company mission.
- *Company implications:* companies that attend to their bigger system are concerned about the world in which they do business. To this end, some insurance companies have 'ethical portfolios' which are committed to investing only in projects that make minimal demands on the world's resources.

Identity

Your identity is a description of *who* you think you are, at any given time and in any given role. It is often conveyed in the labels you give yourself. In many cases, these have a qualitative element, e.g.: 'I am a financial wizard.' As you travel through life, your sense of yourself changes at this identity level and influences some of the options to which you allow yourself to be open. Your identity level can therefore be empowering or restricting of your development. You can enhance someone else's self-esteem by giving them positive feedback at the identity level: 'You are a brilliant organiser.'

At this level you would be answering the question: 'Who am I when I am doing this?'

- *Individual implications:* you will have a number of different identities depending on the context. Think about your identity when you attend a meeting. Are you the chairperson, the minute taker, an expert, a representative, a participant, an observer, an ex officio member, a volunteer, or a combination of some of these? When you go to a family gathering, are you a parent, child, brother, sister, aunt, uncle etc.? Whichever way you describe yourself passes on a message to those around you. It is important that your identity includes a number of different activities.

WHO AM I?

'It's just the way I am.' 'This is how God intended me to be.' There is often a quite fixed sense of self behind these statements. Some people are frightened that a new identity might fundamentally alter their perception of themselves or others' perceptions. This of course ties in with their beliefs too.

- *Company implications:* the company identity gives employees and customers a clear idea of what to expect from the company. Where there is a strong figurehead as founder, that person will often incorporate their identities and values into the company.

  There is sometimes a challenge when an identity presented to the customer is not applied to staff. 'A company that cares … ' may not be consistent in its treatment of its staff. This can percolate through to the way staff treat customers, and the company identity then becomes meaningless. Working with neuro logical levels can uncover these inconsistencies.

  There are obvious implications in mergers and take-overs. The new company needs to have a clear identity to share with the amalgamating groups. Staff at all levels can fear being 'taken over' and pushed into an alien identity. If the new identity is discussed and considered as part of the merger package, it can make the transition much smoother.

Beliefs/values

On Monday, we considered the influence of beliefs on the way you think, your feelings and how you behave as a result. At the neuro logical level of beliefs, you are working with what you believe to be true, and this forms the basis for daily action. Some beliefs are handed down through families and go unchallenged from generations. These can take the form of 'sayings', and they are very powerful. 'You can't teach an old dog new tricks', 'If it tastes bad, it's doing you good', 'Learning happens everywhere', 'Life begins at 40.' Can you think of any that are still around for you? Are they helpful or ready to be jettisoned?

Your *values* are the criteria against which you make decisions. They are the attributes that are important to you in the way you live your life. These could include: loyalty, liberty, honesty. Your beliefs support and reinforce your values. You have to believe that you can change in order to make changes at any of the neuro logical levels.

At this level, you would be answering the question: 'Why am I doing this?'

- *Individual implications:* beliefs can promote or inhibit personal growth. Henry Ford is reported to have said: 'Whether you think you can or whether you think you can't, you're probably right.' Many beliefs are conveyed in thoughts, and they represent your opinion more than firm facts. You tend to notice information that reinforces them and to delete the opposite view.
- *Company implications:* have you ever noticed the passion and zeal in brand new companies? People here may work exceptionally long hours for relatively little financial gain. The rewards they are getting stem from the firm and shared belief in what they are doing. There is a captivating energy that maintains momentum. As with identity, it is important that the company's beliefs about customers as human beings should also be reflected in the beliefs about staff.

There are many limiting beliefs around in the area of new technology. People who for years have managed with a typewriter or secretarial assistance now find a PC on their desk. The beliefs that might stop them from using the machinery are based on a lack of confidence or fear of the new: 'I can't work machines', 'It's too complicated, I'll break it', 'I'm too old to learn.' Contrast these with: 'I thrive on anything new', 'I can handle it.' A company's values provide the codes of practice for the workforce, for example equal-opportunities and environmental policies. There is obvious discord when the company displays such policies but doesn't believe or practise them.

Capabilities
Your *capabilities* are the resources that you have available to you as skills and qualities. These may be formally recognised through standards, qualifications and competencies, and will be demonstrated by the *strategies* you use. Many of your capabilities are processes that you perform regularly, and in many cases they are automatic and habitual.

At this level, you would be answering the question: 'How am I doing this?'

- *Individual implications:* having learned a new set of skills, you might want to consider how you incorporate these. It is great to return from a counselling skills course fired with enthusiasm. If you insist that everyone tell how they feel all the time, they may react in a negative way. You are only part of the way to absorbing the capability that ensures appropriate use of your counselling skills.
- *Company implications*: companies that want to restructure in some way will succeed if they have considered and attained the necessary capabilities on the way. It may seem a small jump to go from being a photographic studio specialising in portraits to a retail film developer. Although you may be able to develop your own pictures, you also need to know how to handle different types of films and different customers. Your accounting skills and staffing needs will be different.

Behaviours

Your *behaviours* are what you do, what you say and what those around you observe or hear. They are the external representation of your capabilities, beliefs, identity and connectedness. On Sunday, you considered outcomes and how to achieve these. One section described being specific. This is very important at the behaviours level. If you have an outcome to aim for, you will be greatly helped by considering the actions you will take to get there. The Chinese have a saying: 'The longest journey starts with the first step.' Behaviours can be easily learned through copying significant *role models* around us. Modelling (which we will discuss on Saturday) is one of the key NLP skills, and was used as a major part of NLP's creation. Bandler and Grinder wanted to know *what* the key therapists *did* that made them excellent.

At this level, you would be answering the question: 'What am I doing?'

- *Individual implications:* what do you do to achieve your outcomes, both personal and work-related? You can set yourself behavioural tasks that will enhance your development. You might decide to volunteer and take minutes at the next team meeting, or to make a tricky phone call that everyone is avoiding.
  Behaviours are sometimes confused with identity and capability, which can damage a person's confidence and competence. Failing an exam doesn't mean that you are stupid or useless at studying, but if it is taken at those levels, you are unlikely to seek feedback as to how you can improve. When you are giving or receiving feedback, consider it at this level of what you do, not at the identity level – who you are. 'You failed this exam and you have passed many other testing situations in your life.'
- *Company implications:* companies behave in many different ways to let the outside world know they exist. They conduct market research surveys and advertising campaigns, they sponsor local charities and send out promotional material to prospective and existing customers. There are set or agreed behaviours that need to be actioned for many company procedures, from allocating petty cash to promotions. These behaviours are lovingly referred to as *red tape*.

Environment
This refers to everything that is outside you: where you are, the people you are with, your home, your work – your surroundings.

At this level, you would be answering the questions: 'Where and with whom?'

- *Individual implications:* your choice of where to live will be influenced by your identity. If you have to move, you would also consider environmental-level factors such as schools, public transport, green space, distance from friends etc. Where you go and what you do socially can all be considered at the environment level.
- *Company implications:* the comfort and safety of your surroundings make a big difference to how well you work and how satisfied you are. Considerations at this level could include: who you lunch with, how you are as a co-worker and your effectiveness in an open- or closed-plan office. Many people will tolerate a poor working environment if they have good relationships with their work colleagues.

Example: the table shown illustrates how someone may describe their desire for change. Read the words and note the implications: these give you a broad idea of which levels would benefit from change. In the example, a nurse is describing his dissatisfaction with work at each level. The questions in italics are ones that might facilitate his change.

In this example, you could help the nurse at any of the neuro logical levels. The six levels are interactive and influence each other. Changes at one level will effect change at the levels below, but changes on the lower levels will not automatically cause change at the higher levels. If he were to change and believe he was good enough, he would acknowledge that his skills were valid, he would behave differently and he would be able to move on in the way he needed.

Neuro logical levels	I don't enjoy nursing anymore.
Purpose	I don't know why I am doing this anymore. *What were your reasons for becoming a nurse?*
Identity	I don't like the person I become when I'm nursing. *Who do you want to be when you are nursing?* *How might you become a person you do like?*
Belief	I don't believe I'm good enough anymore. *How were you good enough in the past? What would make you believe you are good enough now?*
Capability	I need to update my training. *How could you do that? How do other qualifications and experience count?*
Behaviour	I don't have enough time to do all I need to. *What do you have enough time for? What do you do well?*
Environment	It might just be this area. *Is it this specialism, this ward or this hospital?* *What are the hospitals like in other areas?*

Think about an issue that is not right for you at present. In which level is it based? Where might you start to intervene? Once you start to ask yourself the right questions, you may find you move around the levels. How much change or development do you want? Take time to notice whether you have certain levels at which you prefer to operate – how do these compare with colleagues'? If you work in a team where there is friction, it may be that each team member has different ideas at the values or beliefs levels, and that these need sorting.

Reframing

In NLP terms, a *frame* is the focus of attention you give to
something. If you look at a picture from one side, it may
appear quite different than from another perspective. The
value of *reframing* is in being able to consider an issue from
many different aspects. If you have ever put a picture or
photograph into a new frame, you will know how much
that can alter it. That is what you can do with behaviours
or thoughts that seem stuck.

Reframing is a way of getting people to say: 'How else can
I do or consider this?'

Context reframing
Context reframing enables you to recognise that there is a
positive place for almost any behaviour – doing the right
thing in the right place at the right time. Embarrassment is
sometimes the result of just getting the time or place
wrong. Next time you find yourself or someone else
limiting themselves with phrases like, 'I'm too sensitive, too
careless, too slow', or 'I wish I could stop doing … ', use
reframe questions to find a context in which the behaviour
is appropriate and positive:

Question: 'When would it be beneficial to be sensitive?'
Answer: 'When I notice someone in the office who is
nervous or unsure.'

Question: 'Where would being slow be an advantage?'
Answer: 'In a meeting that is making decisions about
budgets.'

Content reframing

Content reframing is where you change the meaning of a seemingly limiting behaviour.

You might want to use content reframing next time you hear statements like: 'My mind goes blank when I stand up to make a presentation', or 'I get upset when I make mistakes.' Your aim is to find another, more useful meaning.

Question: 'What else could going blank mean?'
Answer: 'It could mean I'm clearing my mind to concentrate on what I want to say.'

Question: 'What is the value of getting upset?'
Answer: 'It shows how much pride I take in doing a job well.'

Summary

Today we have focused on change. With the neuro-logical-levels model, you were able to understand how the different levels of thinking interact. The model gives you a framework with which to organise and gather information in order to identify the best point for intervention and to make or suggest changes. In addition, the technique of reframing challenges limiting behaviours, working from the premise that 'choice is better than no choice.' Tomorrow we will consider some techniques to increase your motivation and personal resources.

Increase your options

Wouldn't it be good if you could change the way you approach and react to a variety of different situations, instead of feeling there is nothing you can do about them and telling yourself: 'That is just the way things are.'? One way to increase your options is to give more attention to what *works* in your life and concentrate on that rather than being stuck with what doesn't work. If you have been successful, confident and motivated in any aspects of your life, then you can use those experiences to be so again in many situations of your choice. Today we will look at three widely used NLP techniques to enhance your flexibility before outlining where you might go next.

Submodalities

On Tuesday, we considered representational systems and how these are an expression of the way we think and process information. Within each of these systems, we can now make finer distinctions which give us more data about the quality of our experiences. In NLP, these distinctions are called *submodalities*, and they describe how we refine our sensory experiences. They are the foundation stones of the senses, characterising how each picture, sound and feeling is composed.

Submodalities are how we code experiences and distinguish different sensory systems.

Submodalities make the difference between an experience you remember as positive and one which you'd rather forget or which makes you cringe when you recall it. Once you recognise your preferred method of coding, you can choose whether or not to change the code. This is particularly useful when you want to replace an unmotivated state with a more motivated one, or to lessen the impact of a painful past event. Some people tend to store their memories in a way that leads to negative, low-energy reactions, or to anticipate future events with worry and anxiety. By changing their submodalities, they can alter their whole experience.

What is different about those days when you just can't seem to get out of bed and those when you're up bright and early, raring to go? Some people see the day ahead as dark and cold, and all they can hear is a morbid drone. On the other hand, on their good days, everything is brighter, they feel full of energy and they enjoy listening to the birds singing sweetly. Once you recognise the words that describe your 'good' days, you can choose how to use them.

- Think about a task that you don't like. As you do so, notice whether you recall pictures of the task, the words or sounds associated with it or the accompanying feelings.
- Write down or tape-record a description of what came into your mind, and be as detailed as you can.

Stop thinking about that experience, move around and think of something else.

- This time, think about a task you really enjoy and take on with vigour. As you do so, notice whether you recall pictures of the task, the words or sounds associated with it or the accompanying feelings.

- Write down or tape-record a description of what came into your mind, and be as detailed as you can.

Stop thinking about that experience, move around and come back to now.

- Compare the lists and notice what kind of words you have used to describe your motivated and unmotivated states.

Which submodalities are the difference which makes the difference?

What you have now is an indication of the way your thinking about a situation can make it pleasurable or not. If you accept that a memory is simply that – an event that happened and cannot be changed – why spend time wallowing in the bad moments and letting them influence the way you run your life? By changing your submodalities, you can change the impact and meaning of your thoughts. You can also change your approach to any outstanding tasks.

Your submodality distinctions may have included:

Visual:

- in colour, black and white or shaded
- brightness: dull or shiny
- clarity: dim and hazy, or sharp and in focus
- size: larger than life, lifesize or smaller
- framed or panoramic
- location: in front, to one side or behind you
- clarity: blurred or in focus
- *associated,* i.e. seen through your own eyes, or *dissociated*, i.e. looking at yourself in the picture

Auditory:

- volume: loud or quiet
- words or sounds
- stereo or mono
- distance: close or from afar
- speed: fast or slow
- tone: soft or harsh, and whose voice(s)?
- speed: faster or slower than usual

Kinaesthetic:

- pressure: hard, soft or a sense of being pushed
- texture: rough or smooth
- weight: light or heavy
- location: where in your body do you experience sensations?
- shape: angular or curved
- intensity: strong or weak

- Go back to the task that was not one of your favourites.
- As you think about it this time, consciously make it bigger and closer to you. Imagine yourself doing it rather than watching on from the outside. Use a positive tone of voice to tell yourself how good it will be when you have done it. Imagine feeling satisfied, with a great sense of achievement.
- Play around with *your* submodalities and notice the way they change the impact on you.

You can make changes in any situations. If you don't like the result, change the submodalities back or try something different.

There are some general trends in the submodalities connected with feeling confident and motivated. Pictures here tend to be associated, big and bright. Sounds are clear and normal pace. Feelings will be solid and warm. The way we talk about our inner thoughts also reflects our mood, and thus 'I always look on the bright side', for example, is preferable to 'The future looks black.'

Next time you are thinking about a painful or unpleasant memory, make the picture dark, small and far away from you. Change the voices to comic ones like Donald Duck, and change the music to honky tonk. Then notice the difference in the way you relate to it.

Anchors

In NLP terms, an *anchor* is any stimulus which evokes a consistent response. This can be practical – e.g. the sound of a fire alarm which means 'Stop what you are doing and move outside' – or emotional – e.g. a photograph of a loved one which makes you feel happy and valued. The power of anchors is based on our ability to learn by making links and forming associations. Once established, they become automatic responses which can be beneficial or detrimental to you. The beneficial anchors are those that trigger resourceful states like confidence, energy and creativity. The detrimental anchors activate unresourceful states like depression or frustration and lethargy.

For example: you've had a stressful day at work. You get into your car or onto the bus or train and put on your 'soothing' music tape or take a favourite route. This will calm you down, possibly slow you down and alter your stressed state into a more congenial one. On the other hand, you could get into your car, bus or train, and go over in fine detail all the elements of the meeting that stressed you. You might sit down with a thud, grip the steering wheel tightly, or clutch your briefcase and newspaper tightly and glare at anyone who considers sitting near you. This will keep you fired up and speeded up. I wouldn't want to be the next person to meet you!

What works for you?
If you are nervous or apprehensive about making a presentation or team briefing (or anything you still have to do), you can now choose resourceful anchors to change your approach. The good news is that if you accept the NLP principle discussed on Sunday, 'We have all the resources we need', then you can transfer what you do well and resourcefully from one part of your life to any other part of your life that you choose. You may feel highly creative when decorating your home, and now you can take that creativity into presentations, report writing or negotiations that you handle.

Think of a situation at work or outside where you would like to be more resourceful. Then decide which resource(s) you need to become so – e.g. confidence, calm, energy, concentration or humour.

Locate the resource

Think about a time in the past when you have fully experienced that state you wish to draw upon. It doesn't matter how long ago or whether it was in your professional or personal life. Relive the experience now, seeing the people and things around you as you did at the time. Hear the sounds again, the voices, other noises or maybe the silence. Savour the positive feelings which accompany the experience. Make sure that you are fully associated into the experience, not an onlooking observer. As you recall the resourceful time, you may notice physiological changes too which indicate a sense of well-being. Enjoy this intense feeling of being in your chosen state.

Choose your anchor(s)

You may prefer a visual anchor like a particular scene, person or object. An auditory anchor would include sounds, music or voices, and a kinaesthetic anchor could involve a gesture to recreate the emotions, sensations and feelings. To create a very powerful trigger, you may choose to have all three available. You may see a riverside scene, hear the word 'relax' and squeeze your fingers together to switch yourself instantly into a relaxed state. Do you have a lucky outfit or interview suit? These are anchoring you kinaesthetically because you feel confident and comfortable in them. They are also visual anchors because you like the way you look in them. If they are very bright, they could also be 'loud' auditory anchors!

Decide what your anchor will look, sound or feel like. Make it different from your regular behaviour so that you don't confuse it with other states and resources. Also, choose something discreet that no-one else will notice.

Putting them together
Return to the resourceful time in the past. Re-experience it
again and connect with being there. When the feeling is strong
and reaching its peak, implement your anchors. See the
picture, hear the sound and feel the gesture. Hold them for a
few moments and then release them. Then shake yourself or
move in some way to bring yourself back to the present.

Test it
Remember the initial situation in which you wanted to be
more resourceful? Think about it now, and as you do so, fire
your anchors when they will be most useful as you go
through the situation. How did you react? Has your
thinking about the original situation changed? Notice that
you can now switch to a more resourceful state instantly.
Anchoring is a skill which needs practice. It becomes easier
and more effective the more you use it. The more you use it,
the more it will become part of your unconscious behaviour.
Notice those that already work for you and aim to increase
them. Notice also how you anchor unresourceful states like
bad moods and debilitating anxiety. Change the anchors
and observe what happens. With resource anchoring, you
can increase your emotional choice.

Modelling

As we noted on Sunday, NLP itself was conceived by
working out how excellent therapists communicated with
their clients. Bandler and Grinder did not 'become' Satir,
Erickson or Perls, they learned how to think like them,
modelled them and then applied that thinking to NLP.

Modelling is the process of understanding the thoughts and actions that enable someone to accomplish a task excellently.

Children learn much of their early behaviour through modelling the people around them. It is not surprising that many will share any key interests or hobbies that their parents enjoy. There is a saying: 'Imitation is the sincerest form of flattery', and people do indeed want to be like the people they admire. NLP is not suggesting you can become someone else, just that you if you can understand what makes them achieve so much, then you can model it yourself and then apply your learning to increase your effectiveness.

Great achievers, particularly in sport, will often claim that they modelled themselves on a childhood hero in the same field. They watched how they perfected their game, noticed how they walked or ran and imagined how it would be when they were like their hero.

The modelling process
There are three parts to the full NLP modelling process:

1 *using the 2nd position of the perceptual positions discussed on Monday.* This involves studying the behaviours of the person you want to model and understanding as nearly as possible their map of the world. Ask the question: 'What would I have to do to think and behave like you – as if I were you?'

2 *testing the model by taking out one element at a time as you use it.* Notice the effect: does its removal make any difference? If no, you don't need it. If yes, then you have identified an essential element.

3 *Designing a way to teach the skill to others.* This has clear implications in an organisational setting. You can study the excellent staff in any section and, through coaching and mentoring, pass on the relevant strategies to enhance the skills of the relevant personnel.

Observations and key questions
- Identify the skill you want to model and reproduce. (You can model yourself and transfer an effective strategy of your own into different settings.)
- Select a person or people who demonstrate excellence in this skill.
- Observe and identify:
  - their behaviour – what they do and how they do it
  - their representational systems and body language (Tuesday)
  - their filters and metaprograms (Thursday)
  - their neuro logical levels (Friday)

- Where possible, it is most useful to interview your model to obtain a clear understanding of what they do. Don't be surprised if they are not clear: they will probably do a lot of it unconsciously. If, for example, you wanted to know how someone successfully negotiated a pay rise, ask:
  - 'What do you think about before you go to see your manager?'
  - 'How do you help yourself feel confident?'
  - 'What sorts of questions do you prepare, and how many do you have?'
  - 'How would you describe yourself in the situation?'
  - 'How do you prepare to compromise?'

Next steps

This book has given you the basic tools for understanding Neuro-Linguistic Programming. Although they are derived from a combination of NLP thinkers, by definition, they represent my map of the NLP territory. With NLP, you can increase your choices about how you feel and react in any situation, extending your repertoire in communications with others. It is up to you where you go next.

You may want to go back and assimilate the ideas you have read about, or experiment further with the exercises. Please change any of them so that they make best sense for you. You might decide that you would like to take a course or study further.

Know your outcome

If you have some ideas about your future with NLP, this is also an opportunity to revisit the questions related to outcomes from Sunday – see page 16.

Be flexible

Try out lots of different behaviours and techniques to find out the kind of responses you get. Notice the way other people are thinking and the words they use. Practise the exercises with friends or colleagues. Some may take longer than others to fully comprehend. Start with those that first caught your eye, sounded good or just felt right.

If what you're doing isn't working, do something else.

Further study

Read some of the other authors (listed over) for yourself to broaden your map. Listen to audio cassettes or enrol for a training course. There are plenty of options available.

> You can find out more by contacting:
>
> | Association of NLP | International NLP |
> |---|---|
> | Help Desk | Trainers Association |
> | PO Box 5 | (INLPTA) |
> | Haverford West | PO Box 288 |
> | SA63 4YA | Fareham |
> | www.anlp.org | PO16 0YG |
> | Tel: 0870 7871978 | Tel: 013292 85353 |

Whatever you do next … enjoy getting to know yourself and making sense of what makes you the unique person you are.

> *IN*FORM Training & Communication, an award-winning partnership, provides a professional and client-centred range of services. Visit www.inform-global.com for further information about coaching, training, consultancy and accompanying products.

Further reading

Alder, H. (1996) *NLP for Managers: How to Achieve Excellence at Work*, Piatkus.

Bandler, R. (1997) *Using Your Brain – for a Change*, Real People Press.

Bandler, R. and Grinder, J. (1985) *Frogs into Princes*, Real People Press.

Knight, S. (1995) *NLP at Work: The Difference that makes the Difference in Business*, Nicholas Brealey Publishing.

McDermott, I. and Jago, W. (2001) *The NLP Coach*, Piatkins

McDermott, I. and O'Connor, J. (1997) *Practical NLP for Managers*, Gower.

Molden, D. (1997) *Managing with the Power of NLP for Competitive Advantage*, Pitman Publishing.

Molden, D. (2001) *NLP Business Masterclass*, Financial Times Prentice Hall

O'Connor, J. and Seymour, J. (1997) *Introducing NLP*, 2nd edition, Thorsons.

Robbins, A. (1997) *Unlimited Power*, Simon and Schuster.

Shapiro, M. (2001) *Shift Your Thinking Change Your Life*, Sheldon Press